ISLAM

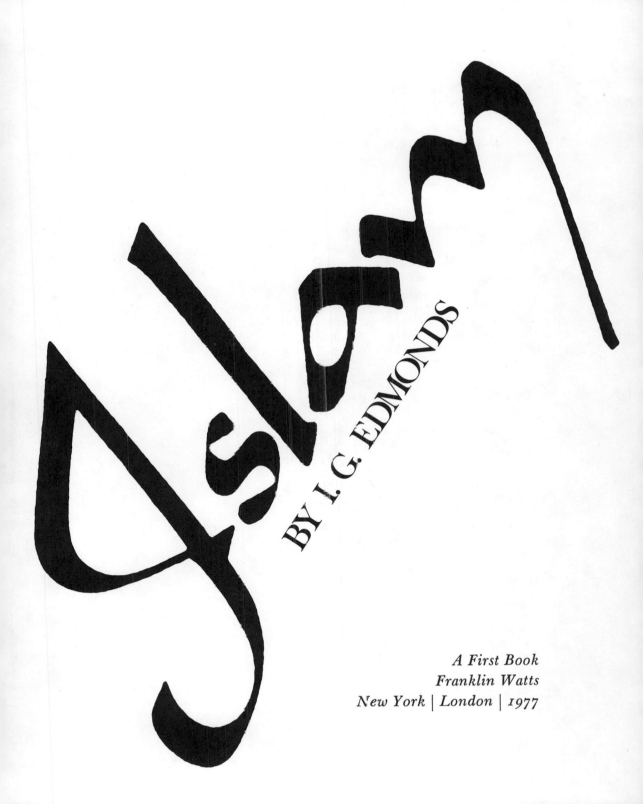

Islam

BY I. G. EDMONDS

A First Book
Franklin Watts
New York | London | 1977

Frontispiece: the gold domed Mosque of Omar, covered with blue, green, and white mosaics, was built in the tenth century to commemorate the visit of Caliph Omar to Jerusalem. It is inside the old walled city. Facing page 1: this window, which uses Arabic writing as part of its design, is in the Shah Mosque in Teheran, Iran.

Photographs courtesy of:

Arab Information Center: frontispiece, 4, 12, 46, 49; I. G. Edmonds: opposite p. 1, 7, 11, 22; Food and Agriculture Organization: p. 6 (left); United Nations: pp. 6 (right), 57 (left); Saudi Arabian Educational Mission/Aramco: pp. 17, 52; University of Edinburgh Library: p. 20; New York Public Library Picture Collection: p. 35; John Bonar-Middle East Communications: p. 57 (right).

Cover design by Beehive Studio, Inc.

Library of Congress Cataloging in Publication Data

Edmonds, I G
    Islam.

    (A First Book)
    Bibliography: p.
    Includes index.
    SUMMARY: Introduces the history, principles, and customs of Islam including the life of Mohammed, a discussion of the Koran, and the influence of Christian and Judaic beliefs.
    1. Islam—Juvenile literature. [1. Islam] I. Title.
BP161.2.E34   297   77–2664
ISBN 0–531–01288–3

CONTENTS

THIS IS ISLAM

Islam is the religion of over 500 million people. Islam means "submission to God." A person who believes in Islam is a *Moslem* (sometimes spelled Muslim), or "one who has given himself to God."

Islam began in Arabia in A.D. 622. Today it has spread far beyond the land of its birth. In addition to the Middle East, where it started, Islam is now the main religion of Turkey, North Africa, Malaysia, Pakistan, Bangladesh, Indonesia, and parts of the Philippine Islands. There are also about 60,000 Moslems in the United States, not including the *Black Muslims*.

Christians and Jews who learn about Islam for the first time are often surprised to find that Abraham, Moses, Jesus Christ, and others from the Judaic and Christian religions are also important to Moslems.

This proves not so surprising when one learns that Islam

draws from the beliefs of Judaism and Christianity. The Prophet Mohammed, who gave Islam to the world, taught that God sometimes sent messengers to inform people of God's will. Abraham, Noah, Moses, David, and Christ, according to Mohammed, were the greatest of these early messengers of God.

As time passed, the messages of these prophets became blurred. Mistakes crept into religious books and teachings. Then, according to the teachings of Islam, God—whom Moslems call *Allah*—sent the last and greatest of his Messengers, Mohammed, to restore the true word of God and to provide a way of salvation for all who accept the creed that "there is no God but Allah and Mohammed is his Messenger."

Many Westerners call Islam "Mohammedism" because Mohammed was its founder, just as Christianity holds sacred the name of its founder, Christ. Moslems point out that this is against the teachings of Mohammed. It suggests that they worship Mohammed, which is not true. Mohammed said that he was not divine. He was a man chosen by Allah to bring Islam to the world.

Islam is a simple and moral religion. It does not demand impossible goodness of its believers. It establishes an easily understood code of laws that the average believer can follow.

Islam also teaches that all believers are equal. There are no priests and no one has special access to sacraments. It teaches a strong sense of community, of belonging to a body of faithful dedicated to submission to God.

Although Jews and Christians will find much that is familiar in Islam, they will also find much that is different. Mohammed kept the basic moral codes of the other two religions. The Moslem hell is also similar, but the idea of heaven is quite different. There are other major differences as well.

[2]

These will be explained as we go deeper into the world of Islam.

"COME TO PRAYER! COME TO PRAYER!"

Moslems call their temples of worship *mosques,* or "places of kneeling." Each mosque has one or more tall, slender towers called minarets. In the old days a bearded man in a long robe and a green turban climbed to a circular balcony on top of the minaret. There he cupped his hands to make a trumpet for his voice. His words, spoken in a deep voice, announced:

> *"Allahu akbar, Allahu akbar. . . .*
> God is most great, God is most great. . . .
> There is no God but Allah, Mohammed is his Messenger. . . .
> Come to prayer, come to prayer."

This man is a *muezzin,* the "caller to prayer." His duty is to remind all within the sound of his voice that they are required by their religion to pray to Allah five times a day. In some areas the muezzin still climbs the minaret to make his call to prayer, but in many places loudspeakers have been placed on top of the minarets. This permits the muezzin to sound his call without climbing the tall tower.

Islam could well be called the religion of prayer, for in no other faith is such strict emphasis placed on regular and frequent prayer. A true Moslem prays five times a day. The Mos-

The Al Azhar Mosque in Cairo has
a minaret in the traditional style.

lem's prayer is an admission of submission to Allah. More often than not, the prayer is a simple plea to God to "help me serve thee better."

THE MOSQUE

The mosque is a place of and for prayer. Sermons may be preached there, and are usually done so at the Friday gatherings. Friday to Moslems is what Saturday is to Jews and Sunday to Christians.

The real purpose of the mosque is to serve as a sacred place where the faithful can pray as a group. But it is not essential to pray in the mosque. The nomad can spread his prayer rug on the desert sand. The businessman can fall on his knees in a back room. The housewife can pray in her home. The farmer can pause in his fields to make his prayer.

However, Mohammed said that prayer in a mosque is better than prayer in private. The Prophet believed that group prayer brought the faithful closer together in their religion. It reminds Moslems that each is but one among a great family.

It is not possible for every Moslem to come to the mosque five times a day for the daily prayer. So most prayers are said at work or in the home. However, good Moslems try to go to the mosque on Friday, the Moslem sabbath. Both men and women may attend the same services, but they pray in different sections.

The traditional mosque is built around a large dome. The inside is plainly furnished, although the walls and ceilings may be beautifully inlaid with designs. Frequently these designs are quotations from the Koran. Islam does not permit pictures or statues representing men or beasts. An exception to

Although anyone can pray alone, anywhere, group prayer can bring people together in a feeling of kinship. Left: a boy in Algeria kneels on his prayer rug. Right: Moslems in Dakar, Senegal, at prayer in the Grand Mosque.

*A large pool in the courtyard of
the Shah Mosque in Teheran,
Iran, is used for ritual washing
before entering the mosque.*

this is the Shiite (pronounced *SHE*-ite) sect, which is in Iran and parts of Iraq and Yemen. It does permit representational art, but orthodox Moslems consider members of the Shiite sect heretics.

There are no pews inside the mosque. The faithful kneel on the floor or on prayer rugs. They face an alcove—called a *mihrab*—which marks the direction of Mecca, the holy city of Islam. Moslems must always face Mecca when praying.

While it is traditional to say that Moslems face Mecca when they pray, actually they are facing the *Kaaba*. This is a rectangular shrine inside cloistered walls in Mecca. A black stone, in a silver frame, is inset in a wall of the Kaaba. The stone was an object of worship in Mecca long before Mohammed proclaimed Islam. Pagan tradition claimed it came from the sky. Mohammed taught that the archangel Gabriel gave it to Abraham. Some modern scholars agree with the pagan belief. They claim the stone is a meteor that fell in Arabia many centuries ago.

Each mosque usually has a square courtyard with a fountain where the faithful can wash. Moslems must be ceremonially clean before going to prayer.

On the desert where there is no water, nomads are permitted to wash with sand. They must cleanse themselves according to strict religious rules. The cleansing must include hands, mouth, face, nostrils, neck, forearms, and feet.

READING THE KORAN

After the ritual cleansing, Moslems may read the *Koran*, the "Bible" of Islam, in the cloisters of the courtyard as they wait for prayer to begin. If they cannot read or do not wish to read, they may join a group clustered around a reader who recites aloud from the sacred book. These readings will continue until the *imam* enters the mosque.

Imam in Arabic means "in front of," but is usually translated as "leader." The imam is not a minister, priest, or rabbi as other religions understand the words. He is, as his name declares, one who stands in front of the faithful and leads them in prayer.

Inside the mosque and to the side of the niche denoting the direction of Mecca, there is a pulpit called the *minbar*. The imam mounts the steps to this so he can face the assembled people.

The Prayer of Assembly is performed as a group with the imam leading. They begin by standing erect with hands together. They go through several movements that end when they kneel and bow their heads to the floor.

The complete action is called the *rakah*, or "bowing down." A different number of rakah may be required for different types of prayer. At the Friday Prayer of Assembly, Moslems do two rakah.

The imam may preach a sermon, but this is not a requirement. However, it is usually done. In explanation of why the imam can preach or not, the Turks tell a witty story of their folk hero Nasr-ed-din Hodja, the man who was both foolish and wise at the same time.

It seems that the Hodja got tired of preaching every Friday. So one day he asked the assembly if they knew what he was going to say to them. They replied that they did not. Whereupon the Hodja said that he saw no point in talking of that which they knew not. So he went to take a nap.

The next Friday he again asked if they knew what he

would talk about. They were not to be tricked again, so they rose in a body and said, "Yes."

The Hodja smiled and said, "Why, then, O True Believers, waste time telling what you already know? I shall retire to nap."

There came another Friday, and again the Hodja, as soon as the prayer was over, asked if anyone knew what he was going to preach about. They had answered no and been cheated of a sermon, and then yes and likewise got nothing. This time they were sure they had the Hodja trapped. Half rose and said yes and the other half rose and said no.

Again the Hodja smiled. "Then let the half who know tell the half who do not and I will retire to my nap," he said.

After that the faithful gave up and were content to let the imam preach if he so desired or keep silent if he so chose.

ISLAM'S ARTICLES OF FAITH

Islam is basically a simple religion, although it has been complicated by religious laws developed through the years by the *Ulama* (doctors of religious law).

Islam is based upon the Creed and the Six Articles of Faith. The Creed of Islam is contained in the words which all Moslems are required to recite. These words are intended to show that they acknowledge and submit to God: "There is no God but Allah and Mohammed is his Messenger." The word "Messenger" is sometimes translated as "Prophet," but Moslems prefer "Messenger."

In accepting the Creed of Islam, a person must also accept the Six Articles of Moslem Faith. These are:

[10]

*After praying, two women talk in a mosque in
Isfahan, Iran. In the background are the mihrab,
the niche pointing to Mecca, and the minbar, the
pulpit for the imam when he leads the prayers.*

*Inscriptions from the Koran are part of the elaborate
interior design of the El Rifai Mosque in Cairo, Egypt.*

1. *A belief in God.*

This is a God who is undivided. He rules the universe with absolute control over all. God is almighty, merciful, eternal, and invisible. He cannot be described or pictured. He is the creator of all things.

2. *A belief in angels.*

This is a requirement for all Moslems. To deny the angels is to deny Mohammed himself, for the Archangel Gabriel gave Mohammed the sacred Koran. Allah is surrounded by angels, all of whom have specific heavenly duties to perform. Four archangels rank above all the others. They are Gabriel, Allah's messenger of inspiration; Michael, guardian of the Jews; Israfil, who summons the faithful at the day of Judgment; and Izra'il, the messenger of death. The angels are made of light. They do not eat or drink.

In addition to the other angels, each human being has two recording angels who stand invisible on each side of him or her. The angel on the right records one's good deeds. The angel on the left records one's sins. The good and bad deeds are totaled and balanced on Judgment Day. Only those whose good deeds outweigh their bad deeds are permitted into paradise.

There are also bad angels as well as good ones. Al Shaitan, the devil, is a fallen angel who was cast out of paradise for disobeying Allah. He is the ruler of evil spirits and the tempter who leads the people to sin.

3. *A belief in the scriptures.*

Allah, through Gabriel, gave the Koran to Mohammed. This sacred book corrects those given to Moses (the Torah), to David (the Psalms), and to Jesus (the Gospel). Moslems believe

[13]

that the Koran is an exact copy of an original book preserved in heaven. It is absolute and cannot be changed. It should never be translated, for translation alters the original word of God. The Koran was composed to be recited and achieves its greatest beauty when read aloud. Moslems often gather around a reader and listen to the Koran before going in to prayer at the mosque. In foreign countries where Arabic is not understood, Moslems frequently hire readers familiar with Arabic to read to them in the original tongue of Allah.

4. *A belief in prophets.*

The prophets of the Jewish and Christian faiths are considered to be Moslems. This is because, by the definition of Moslem, they submitted to God. The true believer is required to believe in these prophets (or messengers). However, Moslems believe that they were *early* prophets. Mohammed is the last and greatest of the prophets.

5. *A belief in the Day of Judgment.*

According to Moslem belief, the dead will rise from the graves on the last day of the world. Then they will be judged according to the good and bad entries of their recording angels.

6. *A belief that human life is ordained by Allah.*

This is the doctrine of predestination. It means that Allah has decreed all that will happen. What is to be, will be. However, since human beings cannot know their destinies, they must continue to make their own choices between good and evil and will be judged accordingly on Judgment Day. Thus, when things go badly for good Moslems, they will say with resignation, "It is the will of Allah."

ISLAM'S
RELIGIOUS DUTIES

A Moslem is also charged with five religious duties. Moslems call these the Pillars of Islam because they support their religion. They are:

1. *The Shahabad, or recitation.*

This duty requires a Moslem to recite the Creed in public: "There is no God but Allah and Mohammed is his Messenger."

2. *The Salat, or Daily Prayer.*

This is the duty that requires a Moslem to pray five times a day with his or her face turned toward the Kaaba in Mecca. For the purpose of this duty, a day is considered to be a twenty-four-hour period.

3. *The Zakat, or almsgiving.*

According to the Koran, giving alms to the poor is as important as prayer in the salvation of a person's soul.

4. *The Fast of Ramadan.*

During the ninth month of the Moslem calendar, no Moslem may eat or drink or indulge in pleasures between sunrise and sunset.

5. *Pilgrimage to Mecca.*

All Moslems who are physically and financially able are encouraged at least once in a lifetime to make a pilgrimage to Mecca.

The pilgrimage is not a requirement for salvation, but it brings special merit. The *hajj* (pilgrimage) is older than Islam. Mecca has been a religious pilgrimage city as far back as history records.

THE PILGRIMAGE
TO MECCA

Both men and women may make the *hajj*. However, women must be accompanied by a relative. Women wear a traditional robe reaching from head to foot. They are veiled, but the veil is held out from the face so that the skin is technically uncovered. Men wear a white robe in a manner to leave the right arm and shoulder bare. Women are excused from the obligation to make the pilgrimage if they are unable to find a proper escort.

The goal of the pilgrims is the Great Mosque of Mecca. There is a cloistered courtyard in the middle of the mosque. The Kaaba is in the middle of the courtyard. It is fifty feet (15.4 meters) high and draped in black silk.

After performing their ritual washing, the pilgrims stop at the edge of the courtyard. They touch their heads to the ground twice in prayer. Then they advance and circle the Kaaba seven times as they pray aloud to Allah. It is customary to kiss the famous black stone before departing. Some also kiss the stone at the beginning of the seven circles around the Kaaba.

The Creed, the Six Elements of Faith, and the Five Pillars of Islam are the foundations of the Moslem religion. In addition to these, a Moslem is bound as well by various laws and traditions. These grew from events in Mohammed's life and

The courtyard of the Great Mosque at Mecca.
At the center is the sacred Kaaba, the
most revered shrine in the Moslem world.

from interpretations of the Koran. To understand them properly, we must go back more than 1,300 years ago, when an inspired camel driver became dissatisfied with the pagan religions of the people of Mecca.

THE MESSENGER OF ALLAH

After Mohammed died, Moslem scholars collected the *hadith*—which are personal recollections of those who knew the Prophet. Thus we know far more about Mohammed's life—including intimate details—than about any other founder of a major religion.

We first hear of him as an orphan named Kutam. His father died shortly before the boy was born in A.D. 570. Kutam's mother also died, when he was six. The boy lived with his grandfather until he was eight years old. He then was taken in by his uncle, abu-Talib.

Kutam joined the camel caravans as soon as he was old enough to shift for himself. He traveled from Mecca in Arabia to Syria, Palestine, and even as far away as Egypt.

At first he was a helper. Then he became a camel driver. He was more intelligent than the average camel driver and tried to learn about the habits and beliefs of the people he met in his travels. He was also pious and hard-working.

In time the young man became a caravan leader. His honesty and concern for his work brought him to the attention of a rich widow named Khadijah. She hired him to drive her camels. Kutam was then twenty-five years old. Khadijah was forty. Not long after he was hired, she sent a man to ask him to marry her. Kutam agreed. All accounts agree that it was a happy marriage, despite the fifteen years' difference in their ages.

The marriage to Khadijah helped give Kutam the security and leisure needed for contemplation. He began withdrawing into the seclusion that led to his contact with Gabriel. Equally important, after Kutam received his message from Allah, it was Khadijah who convinced her doubting husband that his vision had indeed been a message from God.

Mecca, where Kutam grew up, had always been a religious city, drawing pilgrims to see the black stone that is now enshrined in the Kaaba. In Mohammed's early years the shrine was associated with three pagan goddesses sacred to the Arabs.

THE PRAISED ONE

One year there were very heavy rains. The Kaaba was damaged by flood waters. The black stone was dislodged. When the shrine building was repaired, there was an argument over which clan would have the privilege of replacing the sacred stone in the shrine wall. Each clan wanted the privilege for its sheikh. They could not agree. Finally they decided to place the choice in the hands of the desert gods. They agreed to give the privilege to the next man who chanced to enter the temple courtyard.

This man was Kutam. He was known for his great piety, and all agreed that the gods had made a good choice. However, Kutam was dismayed. His clan, the Banu Hashem, was a minor

This fourteenth-century Persian painting shows Mohammed replacing the black stone in the Kaaba with the help of the clan leaders.

one among the Quraysh tribe that ruled Mecca. He felt that the clan chiefs would resent his having such a great distinction. At the same time, he felt that they would be even more outraged if he gave the privilege to another person.

So he took his robe and spread it on the ground. He then reverently placed the black stone in the middle of the robe. All the clan leaders were invited to grasp the cloth together and raise it level with the niche where the stone was to be inserted in the wall. Then Kutam slid the stone into place.

The way Kutam made all the rivals have an equal part in restoring the stone was greatly praised throughout Mecca. From that time on he was called Mohammed, which means "The Praised One."

Not long after his adventure with the holy stone, Mohammed became restless. He had grown dissatisfied with the pagan Arabian religions followed by the various sects in Mecca and Medina, another Arabian holy city. During his wanderings with the caravans, Mohammed had made contact with other religions that seemed closer to the truth.

In Mesopotamia, the "Land Between the Rivers," as the Greeks called it (present-day Syria and Iraq), Mohammed met descendants of Jews who had been brought to Babylon when Nebuchadnezzar sacked Jerusalem centuries before.

From these contacts he heard stories of Abraham, Noah, Moses, David, and Solomon. Then further travels north into Syria brought him into contact with Eastern Christianity. Again he heard of these Jewish prophets, along with a new one called Jesus Christ.

Mohammed was impressed by the similarity of the Judaic and Christian beliefs. He was very interested in the idea of one God who controlled all the universe. In the religions he knew

Many Moslems still live as nomads, as their ancestors did in the days of Mohammed. These tribespeople along the Kuwait-Iran border graze their goats and pack animals at a water hole.

there were many gods, all of whom influenced a person's life.

The things Mohammed learned from the Jews and the Christians took root in his mind and grew over a period of years. The differences between Judaism, Christianity, and Arab paganism disturbed him. Why were there similarities and differences when all supposedly spoke of the same heaven?

THE VISIONS
OF MOHAMMED

It was the custom of his tribe, the Quraysh, to withdraw into the mountains during the month of Ramadan (the ninth month) and meditate on religion. One of the *hadith*—the personal recollections of Mohammed set down by those who knew him—tells how the future Prophet made many of these trips into the hills to meditate alone. After each he would go to the Kaaba and walk around it seven times before going home.

Finally, during one of these pilgrimages to a secluded cave on Mount Hira near Mecca, Mohammed had a vision. He thought the archangel Gabriel appeared to him. Gabriel commanded Mohammed to recite.

Mohammed asked what he was supposed to recite. Gabriel replied with words that later went into the Sura of the Blood Clot in the Koran:

> Recite thou! For thy Lord is the most Beneficent,
> Created man from CLOTS OF BLOOD:
> Recite thou! For thy Lord is the most Beneficent,
> Who hath taught the use of the pen;
> Hath taught Man that which he knoweth not.
>
> [Rodwell's Translation]

Mohammed recited the words and Gabriel departed. Mohammed then awoke from his vision, but refused to believe that Gabriel had actually spoken to him. All his life Mohammed had disliked "possessed" people who claimed that they talked with gods and spirits.

One of the *hadith* quotes Mohammed as deciding to throw himself from a cliff, for he was sure that he had gone mad. Halfway up Mount Hira, he was stopped by a voice from heaven. It said, "O Mohammed! Thou art the Apostle of God and I am Gabriel!"

Mohammed looked up and saw the huge image of the archangel Gabriel with his feet astride the horizon. Gabriel repeated his words. Mohammed tried to look away. But everywhere he turned his eyes he saw Gabriel. Mohammed was unable to move. He stood there on the mountainside transfixed.

In the meantime, his wife Khadija was worried because he had not returned. She sent servants to seek him. They found him standing on the mountain slope and realized that he was in a religious trance. They stole silently away.

Later Mohammed came out of his trance. He returned home greatly disturbed. He went to Khadija for comfort, telling her that he was losing his mind. She strongly disagreed. She said that God knew Mohammed's piety, character, and truthfulness. God would never bring madness upon such a good man.

After she soothed Mohammed's troubled spirit, Khadija went to see her cousin Waraqa, who had embraced the Christian faith. Waraqa was impressed. He declared that Mohammed had been visited by the same angel who spoke to Moses.

Later Waraqa told Mohammed the same thing, expressing his belief that Mohammed had been chosen as God's Messenger. Convinced now that he had talked with Gabriel, Mohammed continued to have visions in which he received the word of God. He began preaching in his home. His first converts were his wife, Khadija, and Ali, the small son of his uncle abu-Talib.

As his converts grew, Mohammed in A.D. 613 expanded his preaching to the streets of Mecca. The Quraysh rulers of Mecca paid little attention to Mohammed at first. Then they became alarmed as the number of his converts increased. Religious pilgrimages to the pagan shrine in Mecca were important to the city's prosperity. Mohammed's claims that the pagan gods were false hurt business.

However, Mohammed's uncle abu-Talib was a powerful man. He told Mohammed that he would not listen to the new religion himself, but that he would protect his nephew from his Quraysh enemies. Abu-Talib also did not object when his son Ali became Mohammed's convert. (Ali later married a daughter of Mohammed and founded the Shiite sect of Islam.)

Abu-Talib and Khadija both died in A.D. 619. This was a blow, for Mohammed lost abu-Talib's protection and Khadijah's inspiration. He was devoted to Khadijah and during her lifetime took no other wife, although permitted to do so by Arabian law and custom.

The Quraysh rulers of Mecca began persecuting Mohammed. They stopped short of murder. This would have caused a blood feud with Mohammed's clan. They would have been forced to avenge him under tribal custom.

By 622 Mohammed's teaching had been so widely accepted that the Quraysh were forced to take action against him.

THE FLIGHT
TO MEDINA

Mohammed was warned by his friend abu-Bakr, a Meccan merchant. Abu-Bakr secured camels and the two fled from Mecca. After some delay, Mohammed, and later his followers, went to Yathrib (now Medina), 240 miles (386 kilometers) north of Mecca, where Mohammed had friends.

The Flight to Medina is known as the *Hegira* in Arabic. It is so important in Islamic history that Moslems date time from this year. Thus the year A.D. 622 is the year 1 A.H. (After Hegira) to Moslems.

There were a large number of Jews in Medina. Some thought, because of the similarity of his teachings to parts of Judaism, that he might be the promised Messiah they expected.

Mohammed quickly became both the spiritual and political head of Medina. He made converts quickly because he did not ask the people to make too great a change in their beliefs. They had always prayed to Allah as the most important of the pagan gods. Mohammed asked only that they cast out the others and recognize Allah as the only God.

Mohammed taught them that all Moslems are equal in the sight of Allah. He also insisted upon women's rights in the home and in the control of their own property. He demanded protection for orphans, and hospitality to visitors, prohibited loaning money for interest, and required charity to the poor.

He banned alcoholic drinks and required the faithful to fast during the month of Ramadan. However, he did not require them to live cold, narrow lives as some puritanical Jewish and Christian sects did. He permitted his followers to have up to four wives, but insisted that each wife must have equal treatment.

When he first came to Medina, Mohammed tried to bring the Jews of the city into Islam. He even ordered his followers to face Jerusalem when they prayed. The Jews, however, quickly found out that, instead of being one of them, Mohammed was out to make drastic changes in their religion. They reacted strongly against his claim that the Torah was incorrect and that he had been sent by Allah to correct this and the Christian texts.

Angered by their attitude, Mohammed ordered the faithful to stop facing Jerusalem when they prayed. Instead, they were to face the Kaaba in Mecca.

It was during this period that the idea of the muezzin climbing to a height to issue the call to prayer began. The faithful needed something in those days before clocks to remind them that it was time for prayer. It was suggested that a bell be rung, but Mohammed did not like bells. He settled on the idea of the caller going through the streets with a wooden clapper.

Then Abdallah ibn Zayd, who was close to Mohammed, told Mohammed of a dream he had. In it a ghost clothed in green told him that the proper call to prayer was to repeat three times the words: "Allahu Akbar! Allahu Akbar!"—and so on through the call to prayer as it is spoken today.

Mohammed liked the idea, but refused to act until another follower had a similar dream. Mohammed then appointed the Abyssinian Bilal as the first muezzin because he had a loud voice that would carry farther than any other.

One of the *hadith* tells of a woman who said Bilal used the top of her house to make his calls to prayer because it was the tallest near the mosque. Later it became the custom to build minarets for the muezzin to make his call from.

THE WARS
OF MOHAMMED

Mohammed soon realized that he could not convert all Arabia to Islam simply by preaching. He had to unify the divided tribes into an Arabic nation. To do this he began the first holy war, or *jihad*. He began by raiding Quraysh caravans. The loot strengthened his position and he was soon strong enough to engage in full warfare against the Quraysh in Mecca.

These wars were extremely important in the rapid spread of Islam. Mohammed was victorious from the start, for his men fought with a religious zeal. Defeated tribes considered this ample proof that Allah was on Mohammed's side. The smaller groups joined him eagerly, embracing Islam as they did.

It was not until A.D. 630 that he was strong enough to attack Mecca itself. The year was 9 A.H. as reckoned by the Moslem calendar. Mohammed was confident as he led his troops into the most important battle of his life. But as fate would have it, the battle proved to be bloodless.

The Meccans, faced by a clearly superior force under Mohammed, surrendered without a battle. The Prophet rode his camel into the courtyard of the Kaaba shrine. After circling the black stone, he dismounted, crying, "Allahu Akbar! God is most great!"

Moslems gathered outside took up the cry until it echoed through the city. Mohammed then personally broke all of the hundreds of stone idols set up in the cloisters around the shrine of the black stone. He decreed that never again would any idols or pictures be permitted in any mosque.

Mohammed returned to Medina, which he continued to make his home for the remaining two years of his life. Just before his death in 632 (11 A.H.) Mohammed made a pilgrimage to Mecca. While there he preached a sermon from camelback and then returned to Medina. Shortly after this he became ill of a fever.

THE DEATH
OF MOHAMMED

Under Moslem law a man is required to give equal attention to each of his wives. Mohammed had four at the time, each living in her own house. Realizing he was dying, he asked the other wives to give him permission to stay in the house of Ayesha, the youngest of them. They give their assent.

Ayesha, daughter of Mohammed's old friend abu-Bakr, is the most interesting of the people who surrounded the Prophet in his last years. She was six years old when he married her. She lived with her parents until she was nine and then came to live with Mohammed. Various *hadith* (traditional stories) tell us that she was willful, impudent, and completely spoiled.

It was said that Ayesha put many of the gray hairs in Mohammed's head. There are a number of stories about her in the *hadith*. One is that Mohammed found a pearl necklace in the loot from a raid on a Quraysh caravan. He gave it to Ayesha. Later his conscience hurt him, for he should have shared it with his companions. And even if they gave it to him as his share, he—under his own equal treatment law—should have shared it with all his wives. He asked for it back. Ayesha angrily refused.

[29]

Mohammed died on June 8, 632 (11 A.H.), with his head in sixteen-year-old Ayesha's lap.

In his life Mohammed can be compared to Moses. Each took divided tribes and welded them into a strong nation by bringing them to believe in one all-powerful God.

Many thought Islam would die without Mohammed's strong leadership. Time proved them wrong, for Islam found another strong leader to carry on Mohammed's work.

THE KORAN

The *Koran* is the Moslem Bible. Moslems believe it is the Word of God as dictated to Mohammed by the archangel Gabriel. It is somewhat shorter than the Christian New Testament. The text is divided into *suras* (chapters), which do not follow any set plan. This makes the Koran difficult to read. Translators often rearrange the suras to achieve a better order. This is a practice that horrifies most Moslems. They feel that it is tampering with God's Word.

Allah revealed the Koran to Mohammed through Gabriel. Mohammed in turn revealed the Koran to his followers through sermons and talks. Mohammed could not write and did not encourage his followers to record what he said. He expected the Koran to be delivered by reciters, like the familiar Arabic storytellers who recount folktales in the marketplace.

This worked well enough during the Prophet's lifetime.

He often sent reciters who had memorized his sermons to outlying tribes. Then, two years after Mohammed's death, a number of skilled reciters were killed in a battle with a rebel tribe near Mecca. Abu-Bakr, who had succeeded Mohammed as head of the Islamic religion, feared that the Word might be lost if they continued to depend upon reciters.

He ordered Zaid ibn Thabit, who had been close to Mohammed, to collect a written record of the Prophet's sermons. Zaid searched out all who had known Mohammed. Some told him what they remembered. Others produced notes that they had written after listening to the Prophet. These notes had been scratched on flat stones, scraps of paper, and even palm leaves.

Zaid did not rely on any one source. He wrote down what he was shown or told. Then he checked with others who had heard the sermons. Only when the majority said, "Yes, this is as the Prophet spoke," did Zaid include the material in the written Koran.

Zaid made only one hand-written copy of the first Koran. This was taken by abu-Bakr, but was later given to Ayesha, the Prophet's young widow.

Zaid's Koran contained 114 suras. He did not attempt to arrange the sermons as Mohammed spoke them. He merely put the longest suras first and the shortest last.

DIFFICULTY IN
TRANSLATING THE KORAN

Translators try to rearrange the suras. The reason is that when Mohammed first started to preach in Mecca, he spoke more poetically as he told of Allah's oneness and his mercy to mankind. Later, in the Medina period, Mohammed's style of speaking changed. He was then the political as well as the spiritual head of Islam. He became more concerned with setting forth laws and rules of conduct. His style became less poetic.

In Zaid's arrangement, made according to length of the suras, the abrupt change from the poetic Mecca style to the more matter-of-fact Medina style and back again is jarring. Therefore, translators attempt to put the suras back into the order in which they think Mohammed recited them.

Another reason that translators try to rearrange the suras is that the Koran often refers to events that happened in Mohammed's time. Some of these references are easy to identify. Others are obscure. This makes the exact meaning of some passages difficult to understand. If the suras could be rearranged in the order that Mohammed first recited them, it might be possible to determine the events the passages refer to. No translator has yet found an arrangement that satisfies everyone.

Moslems, of course, object to any rearrangement of the suras. They believe that the Koran is the absolute world of Allah. They also object to translations. A translation is not the original words of Allah as delivered to Mohammed in Arabic.

CORRECTING
THE TRUE KORAN

Zaid's first copy of the Koran was later copied and recopied. The copyists had trouble with obscure passages just as foreign translators do. Each made his own interpretation, so that in time copies of the Arabic Koran differed from each other.

A basic belief of Islam is that Allah had previously given the Word to Moses and Jesus and that this Word was corrupted by improper copying. Allah then chose to restore the True Word by giving the correct book to Mohammed. Now the same thing that happened to the Bible was happening to the Koran. Changes were creeping into the Gospel.

Hadzeifa, a friend of the Caliph Othman (who headed Islam from A.D. 644 to 656), complained that this must be stopped "before Moslems differ regarding their scriptures as do the Jews and the Christians."

Othman agreed. He asked the aged Zaid, who had written down the first version of the Koran, to oversee a rewrite that would be for all time the true book. Zaid assembled twelve learned scholars. Their work became the unchanging Koran that Moslems use today.

SOURCES OF THE KORAN

Moslems believe that the Koran came directly from Allah. Western scholars have devoted much time to tracing the sources of the sacred book. Much of its inspiration came from Jewish and Christian scriptures.

Mohammed probably picked up his knowledge of the original scriptures from talking with people he met in his travels. The Prophet then applied his own beliefs, which were influenced by Arabic traditions. An example of this is the way he retained the Kaaba, the black stone of Mecca, which had been sacred to the pagan Arabian religions.

Mohammed's changes to basic scripture are shown in his treatment of Jesus Christ. He considered Christ a prophet like himself. He denied Christ's divinity, just as he denied his own. Therefore Christ could not have risen from the dead. This is in keeping with the Creed of Islam: "There is no God but Allah."

In the sura called The Night Journey (67) the Koran says: "And say: Praise be to God who hath not begotten a son, who hath no partner in the Kingdom, nor any protector on account of weakness." To admit that God has a son would mean there is more than one God, a violation of the Moslem Creed.

Mohammed wanted to create a religion that all people could believe. He was unable to understand why Christians and Jews failed to see the superiority of Islam. Jews and Christians are referred to in the Koran as "the people of the Book." There are frequent pleas for them to join Islam. In Sura 3 (The Family of Imran) the Koran says:

> O people of the Book!
> why disbelieve the signs of God,
> of which yourselves have been witnesses?
>
> O people of the Book!
> why clothe ye the truth with falsehood?
> Why wittingly hide the truth?

Some scholars believe that the Italian poet Dante may have patterned his *Divine Comedy* after Mohammed's account of his Night Journey to heaven and hell. This may have been true in parts, although the Roman poet Vergil is supposed to have been Dante's original inspiration.

The Night Journey of Mohammed is mentioned in the Koran, but the most complete account is in the *hadith* of ibn-Ishaq. The *hadith,* the collection of stories about Mohammed and those close to him, contain the only known history of Mohammed during certain periods of his life. Some of these are

A fifteenth-century Turkish manuscript illustrates a famous
hadith, *the Night Journey: Mohammed, riding a mare with a
human head, enters the seventh heaven where he meets Adam.*

probably fiction. Moslems do not reject them for this reason, if they contain a moral truth in keeping with Islamic law.

MOHAMMED'S VISIT TO HEAVEN

In ibn-Ishaq's account of the Night Journey, Mohammed's spirit left his body while the Prophet slept. It went with Gabriel to Jerusalem. There Mohammed met Abraham, Moses, and Jesus among a group of earlier prophets.

Later Gabriel provided a miraculous ladder, which he and Mohammed climbed to the lowest level of heaven. Here the cover of hell was raised so Mohammed could see the leaping flames. Then, in the manner of the later Dante, Mohammed saw souls undergoing punishment. Men who had stolen the inheritance of orphans were forced to eat stones of fire. Men who had charged interest on loans were eternally trampled by the hoofs of camels. Other sins were similarly punished.

From the pits of punishment Mohammed climbed to the second level of heaven, where he again met Jesus, in the company of John the Baptist. Finally, in the seventh heaven, Mohammed found Abraham. The patriarch was seated outside the gates of Allah's palace. Abraham took Mohammed into paradise, where good Moslems go after Judgment Day. (Moslems believe that if they are killed fighting for their religion, they go immediately to paradise without having to wait for Judgment Day.)

The Koran, in Sura 45, pictures paradise as "gardens of delight." The faithful recline on couches and are served the finest fruits and wines by beautiful *houri*—young girls who never age. Wine, forbidden to Moslems on earth, is permitted in paradise.

If Dante did draw any inspiration from the Night Journey of Mohammed, he repaid Islam in a poor way. The Italian poet pictured Mohammed in one of the pits of Hell. The Prophet's punishment was having his body split in half. This was symbolic in Dante's mind with Mohammed's "sin" in splitting religion to form a new one.

THE WORLD OF ISLAM

Mohammed dreamed of founding one great religious brotherhood. His failure to bring Christians and Jews into Islam was a disappointment that has already been told. He also failed to make Islam strong enough to prevent it splintering into sects.

Mohammed was a very strong leader. As usually happens when such a man dies, other strong men contest to take his place. The power struggles that followed Mohammed's death finally resulted in dividing the Moslems.

Mohammed's death on June 8, A.D. 632, was a shock to many of his followers. Mohammed had denied that he was divine, but few believed him. He was the Chosen of Allah, the Messenger of God. How, they asked, could such a man die?

When Mohammed died with his head in her lap, Ayesha sent a messenger to inform her father, abu-Bakr. Omar ibn-al-Khattab, who was with abu-Bakr, refused to believe that Mohammed was dead. He loudly proclaimed that Mohammed had gone to heaven and would return as Moses returned after forty days on Mount Sinai.

Abu-Bakr rushed to his daughter's house. He turned back the cloth Ayesha had placed over the dead man's face. He kissed the Prophet and cried, "You shall not die a second death!" By this he meant that the Prophet's teachings would continue. He dedicated himself to this task.

Abu-Bakr then returned to the others. All were resigned to the Prophet's death except Omar. He was still in the street, loudly telling a crowd that Mohammed could not die. Abu-Bakr tried to stop him, but Omar would not listen to reason. Abu-Bakr then called to the crowd around Omar.

"In the name of Allah, the Compassionate, the Merciful!" he cried. "O True Believers, if any man worships Mohammed, Mohammed is dead! If any man worships Allah, Allah is alive, immortal!"

He then quoted from Sura 3 (The Family of Imran) that Mohammed was but an apostle. "No one can die except by God's permission," he added. "Other apostles have passed away before Mohammed. If he dies, or be slain, will ye turn upon your heels and return to worship idols?"

These words, which they had heard Mohammed use, had a strong effect upon the crowd. Omar stopped shouting. He sank to his knees in the dust and bowed toward Mecca.

THE CALIPHS
OF ISLAM

Islam faced a crisis. The proud Quraysh of Mecca—although they had at first been Mohammed's bitter enemies—now felt that one of their members should be the Prophet's *caliph*, or successor. The Medina Moslems claimed the right to provide the caliph because they had fought the Prophet's wars while the Quraysh resisted him.

There was a suggestion that two caliphs be chosen. One would represent Mecca and the other would represent Medina. Abu-Bakr objected strongly. He said this would be the beginning of the break-up of Islam. Mohammed, he reminded them, had worked for a united Moslem world.

Omar then addressed the assembly of Moslem elders. He reminded them that abu-Bakr had given up his business in Mecca to help Mohammed make the hegira to Medina. In addition, he had served the Prophet with great faithfulness since that time. Abu-Bakr was also Mohammed's father-in-law, being Ayesha's father. Omar proposed that the quarreling factions set aside their own ambitions and unite under abu-Bakr. They agreed and elected abu-Bakr First Caliph.

Tribes outside of Medina and Mecca refused to recognize abu-Bakr as their religious and political leader. Abu-Bakr, backed by Omar as his first lieutenant, went to war. The fighting continued for two years before the rebellious tribes were subdued.

After the Arabs were again united, abu-Bakr and Omar gave deep consideration to the future. They considered the political situation in Arabia and in adjacent countries they considered a threat to the Arabs. They also had before them the mandate of the Koran to "make war on the infidels and hypocrites, and deal rigorously with them." They decided to lead a new series of jihad (holy wars). Persia (present-day Iran) was chosen for the first attack.

Abu-Bakr died in A.D. 634. Omar was elected Second Caliph. This was a bitter disappointment to Ali, who argued that the caliphate should remain in the direct bloodline of Mohammed. Ali was the Prophet's closest living male relative. He was also Mohammed's first cousin, the Prophet's son-in-law, and the father of Mohammed's only grandchildren.

Ali swallowed his disappointment. None could find fault with Omar. The invasion of Persia was going well, further uniting the Moslems. Omar's popularity with the people was so great that Ali realized that he could not possibly hope to challenge it.

The choice of Omar as Second Caliph was inspired. He is second only to Mohammed in services to Islam. In his youth Omar was a violent man, but he had the iron will needed to keep the Moslems together.

Originally he hated Mohammed and Islam. Hearing that his sister had been converted, he rushed to her house where he found the girl reading some notes of one of Mohammed's sermons. He beat her unmercifully. Then, picking up the notes to see what heresy they contained, Omar was struck by what he read. He immediately went to Mohammed and pledged his submission to Allah.

Omar ruled as Second Caliph from 634 to 644. Under his leadership, the Moslem army won major victories in Persia in 637, Syria in 634 to 640, and in Egypt from 639 to 642.

Omar did not, as many conquerors did, force his religion upon the people he subdued. They were given a chance to become Moslems. If they did, they had all the rights of the faithful. If they did not, they were usually subject to a tax that was not levied upon Moslems. Many did submit to Allah. Persia (modern Iran), Syria, and Egypt all became Moslem countries and remain so today.

Omar lived a simple life. He was entitled to one fifth of

the battle loot, but gave it all away. He wandered about in old clothes and even mended his own sandals. He died in 644, knifed while at prayer in a mosque by a Persian slave to avenge the Moslem conquest of Persia.

THE THIRD AND FOURTH CALIPHS

The Companions of the Prophet—men who had served under Mohammed—met and elected Othman, another son-in-law of the Prophet, as the Third Caliph. Othman was a very pious man, but he permitted his relatives to have a greater share in war spoils than the rest of the Companions. This caused great discontent. Ali—smarting because he had again been passed over for Caliph—took advantage of this to raise opposition to Othman. Finally in 656 some outraged soldiers forced their way into the palace and killed Othman with their swords. The killers then joined with two other Companions to elect Ali as Fourth Caliph.

Ali was the son of Mohammed's uncle. He was converted to Islam at the age of twelve, the first male convert and, after Mohammed's wife, the second person to embrace Islam. From the time of Mohammed's death, Ali had dreamed of succeeding the Prophet. Counting from the time of his conversion to his election, it took Ali forty-six years to achieve his ambition.

Soon the two Companions who had first supported Ali joined Ayesha, Mohammed's widow, in opposing Ali. Publicly they objected to Ali's belief that the caliphate should be hereditary in Mohammed's family. However, some politics and jealousies seem to have been involved.

Ali struck back by killing the two men. Then Muawiyah,

an army general, claimed blood rights. Othman was his cousin, and he accused Ali of being responsible for Othman's assassination. Under Moslem law he had the right to avenge his kinsman's death.

This set the stage for civil war, but Ali, trying to avoid trouble, came to terms with Muawiyah. This infuriated the more puritanical Moslems. They claimed that violated the Koran by settling without a fight, quoting sura 49, which says if two bodies of the faithful are at war "and if one of them wrongs the other, fight against that party which doth the wrong, until they come back to the precepts of God."

These puritans condemned Ali for failing to fight. They said they would be infidels themselves if they continued to support Ali. They withdrew to form a new sect called the Kharijites. One of their members assassinated Ali in 661.

THE MOSLEM CONQUESTS

Ali was the last of the caliphs who knew Mohammed personally. The new caliphs, however, were just as fervent Moslems and continued the conquests started by abu-Bakr. They carried the banner of Islam into Sind (in present Pakistan), almost captured Constantinople (present Istanbul), and completed the invasion of North Africa.

In 711 they crossed into Spain and then marched over the Pyrenees Mountains into France. The invasion was finally stopped at Tours, 147 miles (236 kilometers) from Paris, by Charles Martel. This is considered one of history's most important battles. If the Moslems had won this battle, they would have won all Europe. Then Islam, instead of Christianity, might have become the dominant religion of Europe. That happened in most of the other countries the Moslems conquered.

During these eventful years, Islam continued to divide into different sects. The three main divisions of Islam continued to be the Sunnites, the orthodox Moslems; the Shiites, who followed the teachings of Ali; and the Kharijites, who disagreed with both of them.

The Shiite followers of Ali differed from orthodox Sunnites in believing that the caliph should be a blood descendant of Mohammed. They also differed in rituals and the call to prayer. The Shiites also reject predestination. They argue that Allah gives a person free choice between good and evil and will judge him or her on the choice made. However, they support the Creed of Islam, the Five Pillars, and the Articles of Faith except for predestination.

In A.D. 750 the heart of the Moslem empire shifted to Baghdad, in present-day Iraq. This was a golden age for the Moslems. It peaked under Harun al-Rashid, the Caliph of the *Arabian Nights.* Art, literature, architecture, and medicine reached a high state of perfection at a time when Europe was slumped in the Dark Ages.

The Moslem culture had originally been Arabic, but it absorbed much from the conquered countries. In time it became not a true empire, but more a commonwealth held together only by a common religion. Beginning in the eleventh century, Christian rulers of Europe united in a series of Crusades intended to drive the Moslems from Jerusalem. The famous Richard the Lion-Hearted of England was a leader of the Third Crusade in the twelfth century.

The Arab Moslem empire was destroyed by the Mongol Genghis Khan in the thirteenth century. Although Genghis

Khan destroyed the Moslem empire, his descendants carried Islam deep into India.

The Arab conquests and trading ships carried Islam throughout the Middle East, North Africa, and Spain. Soon after the death of Mohammed, Arab traders had introduced Islam into the Sind area of India (present-day southern Pakistan). It did not spread beyond this area until the Moslem rulers of Afghanistan began encroaching deeper into India in the eleventh century. These men were of Turki and Mongol origin. In the beginning they were primarily raiders, striking India and retreating back to Afghanistan. Gradually they extended their control as far as Delhi, India, only to be slaughtered in 1398 by Tamerlane the Earthshaker.

Various Moslem conquerors continued to rule parts of north India after Tamerlane withdrew until the sixteenth century, when Baber established the great Mogul empire. *Mogul* is the Indian corruption of *Mongol*. Baber was the fifth descendant of Tamerlane on his father's side and the fourteenth descendant of Genghis Khan on his mother's side.

The Moslem conquest of India points up the great difference between Islam as followed by the Arab conquerors and that followed by the Turki and Moguls. The Arabs lived in peace with their conquered people, permitting them to decide whether or not to join Islam. In India the Moslem rulers, with very few exceptions, thought it their religious duty to persecute and destroy Hinduism.

This intolerance created such bitterness between the two religions that in 1947 it split India to form the Hindu nation of India and the Moslem nation of Pakistan, which later divided into the present Pakistan and Bangladesh. The separation led to atrocities committed by Moslems against Hindus and Hindus against Moslems. The conflict was marked by extreme cruelty and viciousness on both sides.

ISLAM TODAY

Today Islam is one of the world's greatest religions. The numbers vary according to different authorities. *The World Almanac* (1976 edition) lists the total world Moslem population as 529,108,700. In contrast, the Christian religion is listed at 944,065,450, including both Catholic and Protestant denominations.

The bulk of today's Moslems are concentrated in the Middle East, Pakistan, Bangladesh, sections of Africa, Indonesia, Malaysia, and Turkey. The largest concentrations in Africa are in Morocco, Algeria, Libya, Egypt, Sudan, Tanzania, and Nigeria. There are also sizeable groups of Moslems in areas of Yugoslavia, Serbia, Macedonia, and Albania.

Moslems are also found in Russia, India, China, South America, and North America. South America has an estimated 191,000 Moslems. North America has 235,000. Figures on the number in the United States are conflicting, but appear to be about 60,000.

The conflict on the number of Moslems in the United States may be due to some authorities including organizations

*Moslems leaving a mosque
after services in Khartoum, Sudan.*

which profess Moslem beliefs, but which are not recognized by Orthodox Moslems. The Black Muslim movement is one of these.

THE BLACK MUSLIMS

The estimated number of Moslems in the United States does not include the Black Muslim movement. The Black Muslim organization was started in 1930 by Wali Farad, a resident of Detroit, Michigan. Farad taught, or at least his followers believed, that he was Allah, who had come from Mecca to establish the Black Nation of Islam. Farad taught that the Battle of Armageddon, the final battle before Judgment Day, would be fought between blacks and whites.

Farad disappeared in 1934. The mystery of his going has never been solved. Elijah Muhammad (Elijah Poole) became head of the Black Muslim movement and served until his death in 1975.

Although the Black Muslims claim their teachings are based upon the Koran, orthodox Islam does not recognize the movement. One reason is the claim that Wali Farad was Allah. Such a claim is violently rejected by Moslems. Allah, in their view, is invisible and works only through messengers and angels. He must not even be pictured, much less seen by anyone. Also, it is unthinkable in their eyes that Allah would appear to any but orthodox Moslems if he should choose to make himself known.

Another major objection to the Black Muslim movement by orthodox Moslems is the Black Muslims' race consciousness. This is directly contrary to Mohammed's teachings that all

Moslems are brothers. True Islam recognizes all its followers as equal regardless of color or racial origins.

SECTS OF MODERN ISLAM

Basically, modern Islam is divided between the orthodox Sunni sect and the Shiites of the Shia sect. The Kharijites, who were the first to break away from orthodox Islam, have not grown like the other two sects. Their feeling toward the Sunnites is summed up in a statement made by one of their members who said, "Then ruled Muawiyah, son of Abu Sufyan, accursed of God's Messenger, and the son of one accursed. He made farmers of God's servants and a briarpatch of God's religion, so curse him with God's curse."

The Kharijites were equally bitter toward Ali's Shiites, saying. "As for the followers of Ali, they are a group which has repudiated the Book of God. They did not leave the Brotherhood of Moslems because of their deep knowledge of the Koran [as we did]. They are determined upon tumult. They know not the way."

The Sunna sect still hopes to bring all Moslems back under a single brotherhood, but the Kharijites and Shiites are as strong as ever in their opposition. The Sunnites today comprise about 65 percent of Islam, although they have divided into some sub-sects. They are widely located throughout the entire Moslem world, while the Shiites are located mostly in Iran, Iraq, and parts of Yemen.

Although all Moslems accept the Creed of Islam, perform the Five Religious Duties (the Pillars of Islam), and observe most of the Articles of Faith, they are very conscious of their differences from other Moslem sects. In Iran, for example, if

Moulay Idriss, *the religious festival that annually attracts many pilgrims to an important tomb in Morocco. Riding demonstrations are an important part of the celebrations.*

one mentions (as I did) that Ali was the Fourth Caliph, you are gently but firmly reminded that, *"We* call Ali the First Caliph."

The same is true when one comments on other differences. The reply is often, "That is not the way we do it. You are thinking of the Arabs."

The Sunnites, in turn, consider the Shiites heretics.

THE WAHABIS OF ARABIA

The most puritanical Moslems are the Wahabi sect, a branch of the Sunnites. There are only about a half million of them but they are important because they include the ruling class of Saudi Arabia. Saudi Arabia, because of its enormous oil reserves and tremendous income, is the second most important Moslem country in the world today. It is surpassed only by Iran in importance in the Middle East.

The Wahabi sect was formed by Mohammed ibn-Abd-al-Wahab, who objected to the *Ijma* of the Sunnites. Ijma is one of the four sections of Islamic religious law.

The first section of the law is legislation from the Koran. This includes all the laws laid down by Mohammed in the Koran. The second section of the law is the traditions. These are drawn from the *hadith.* Six sections of *hadith* traditions are considered authoritative by the Moslems. They have the effect of laws. The third section is *Qiyas,* or reasoning. This is used when a problem arises for which no answer can be found either in the Koran or in the traditions. The judges depend upon common sense, local customs, and Moslem principles to arrive at a just decision.

The fourth section of Moslem religious law is ijma, or "scholarly consensus," which means the opinion of the majority. Ijma is based upon the tradition that Mohammed once said, "My people will never agree on an error of faith." Therefore, if a question arises that cannot be solved by any of the other three laws, a college of scholars is assembled to consider the problem. The opinion of the majority is as binding as the Koran.

Al-Wahab could not agree with this. In his view the Koran was the supreme and only law. He attracted a rather large following, but was persecuted by the orthodox Sunnites. The powerful Saud family came to his aid in 1747. After al-Wahab died in 1792, the Sauds took over leadership of the sect.

The Sauds were overthrown by the Ottoman Turks and it was not until after World War II that they regained power under the great Ibn-Saud. Ibn-Saud conquered most of the Arabian Peninsula and renamed his kingdom Saudi Arabia in memory of his family.

The Sauds clung to their Wahabi faith during their long years of misfortune. Today Wahabi doctrine is the basis of Saudi Arabian law. The custom of cutting off a thief's hand, approved by the Koran, is still enforced. Slavery, also condoned by the Koran, is still followed in Saudi Arabia. However, one Moslem may not enslave another. Owners must treat slaves kindly, and those who give slaves freedom are praised.

The Koran's prohibition against alcoholic drink is not rigidly enforced in some Moslem countries, but it is in Saudi Arabia. In countries such as Egypt and Turkey civil courts have replaced religious law courts, but not in Saudi Arabia.

The Wahabis do not even permit monuments on graves. In 1975 a deranged prince, concerned over modernization, which he considered a violation of the Koran, assassinated King Faisal. Although King Faisal was an important person, he was

*School boys in Saudi Arabia, which officially practices
a very conservative interpretation of Islam.*

buried in an unmarked grave just as his father, the great Ibn-Saud, had been.

In the past, Moslems had never been strong missionaries. Islam was spread through the Middle East, North Africa, Turkey, India, the Balkans, and sections of southern Russia by conquest. In most cases, Islam was not forced upon the conquered people. They embraced Islam because, since it was simple, they could understand it better than some of their own religions; because—in some cases—they could escape the tax on non-Moslems; and because, being the religion of a conqueror, it was obviously more powerful than their own.

In Malaysia, Indonesia, and parts of north-central Africa, Islam was spread by Moslem traders. In India, Islam had an appeal to the lower classes in the areas now known as Pakistan and Bangladesh. India had the caste system, and a person could not rise above the level he or she was born into. Islam teaches that all people are equal. This appealed strongly to lower-caste Hindus.

While Arabic conquerors treated the local people with considerable tolerance, the Moslem Moguls who ruled India were often exceptions. Some grew to repent their persecutions later, like Akbar the Great, who ruled Hindustan from 1556 to 1605. Late in life, Akbar said:

> Formerly I persecuted men in conformity with my faith and deemed it Islam. As I grew in knowledge, I was overwhelmed with shame. What constancy can be expected of men forced into a religion? If men walk in the way of God's will, interference with them would be a crime in itself. If they do not believe in God, they are sick with ignorance and deserve my pity.

The mystic Sufis were the only Moslems who were energetic missionaries. The Sufi movement was a reaction to the rich life that Moslem conquerors lived in the countries they overran. The Sufis were ascetic monks who wore roughly woven wool robes called *suf,* from which their name came. At one time they were quite widely spread through the Moslem world, but they are very few today. Orthodox Moslems do not approve of the Sufis. They think that Sufi mysticism is tinged with too much Western thought.

In the nineteenth century a more active missionary movement was begun. It continues today. The Ahmadiyya sect of Pakistan sends out missionaries into Europe, America, Asia, and Africa. The al-Azhar University of Cairo, the place of intellectual religious instruction of Islam, is now training Moslem missionaries.

POLITICS AND
THE MOSLEMS

In the eighteenth and nineteenth centuries most Moslem countries were conquered by European colonial powers. Turkey managed to remain independent, but the rest of the Middle East, Africa, including Egypt, and Indonesia were either taken over completely or were dominated by foreign powers.

European control began to break up after World War I and completely disappeared after World War II. Today Moslems are in complete control of many countries and have become a powerful force in world politics and economics.

The world's need for oil is the reason for the extreme importance of Moslem countries today. As the oil reserves of the United States dwindled, discoveries in the Middle East, North

Africa, and Indonesia made the Moslem countries among the world's major oil producers.

Moslems do not divorce their religion from their politics and commercial dealings. This caused a world crisis in 1973. Moslems have always deeply resented the establishment of Israel as a nation in land (Palestine) controlled by Arabs for the past 1,300 years. During the Israeli-Arab war in October, 1973, the Arab oil-producing countries declared a petroleum embargo against the United States and the Netherlands for supporting Israel in the war. Iran—a non-Arabic Moslem country —did not join in the boycott.

However, Iran did join the Arabs in a quadruple increase in the price of oil. This drastic increase in oil prices caused an immediate world recession and made inflation soar. At the same time the Arabs frankly announced that they intended to use Allah's oil as a political weapon in their fight.

The staggering increases in oil prices overloaded the treasuries of the oil-producing Moslem states. This has greatly improved the always low standard of living in these countries. Kuwait, a tiny Moslem country between Saudi Arabia and Iraq, was once one of the most poverty-stricken countries of the world. It now has one of the world's highest standards of living. The country has been described as a pile of sand sitting on top of a sea of oil.

All Moslem countries have not shared directly in this sudden burst of wealth. Bangladesh, on the coast east of India, is one of the world's poorest countries. The Moslem African nations in north-central Africa, outside the oil belt, are also poor. Egypt is also a poverty-ridden country.

The oil-rich Moslem countries, true to the Moslem principle of Zakat (alms-giving) have been quite generous to their less fortunate brothers. After a recent Pakistan earthquake, they rushed aid far in excess of what was needed. Saudi Arabia has also given considerable aid to Egypt and Jordan. However, Kuwait has used part of its oil wealth as a political tool by supporting the Palestine guerrilla movement in its attacks on Israel.

Industrialized countries, which formerly ignored the backward Moslem countries, are now eager to sell their products and arms in the Middle East. This turnabout has brought Islam great prestige with its own followers and among undeveloped countries who have always resented the West.

The economic and international importance of the Moslems is certain to continue to grow. The changing condition is certain to have some effect upon Islam itself. As each country's prosperity increases and as it becomes more Westernized through the influx of luxury goods and foreign ideas, there is certain to be an effect upon Islam. Some of the more rigid rules will be under pressure. We have already seen the religious law courts give way in Turkey and Egypt to civil law courts.

The position of women in Moslem countries has always been subservient, although their lot had been greatly improved by Mohammed from pagan times. Considerable progress in women's rights has been made in Iran and Turkey and to a lesser degree in Egypt. It is unchanged in Saudi Arabia and is not likely to improve in the foreseeable future.

The rate of emancipation of women in the other Moslem countries has been slow. Tradition, lack of education, and very strong ties to their homes have combined to keep them from demanding equality. In most cases, the major advances in recent years have been forced upon them. This happened in Turkey after World War I when Kemel Ataturk almost single-

*Left: these women entering a mosque in Fez, Morocco,
still cover their faces with the traditional veil.
Right: this young man and woman study at
the co-educational University of Jordan.*

handedly attempted to force the populace to stop living in the past.

In 1935 Reza Shah, the father of the present Shah of Iran, had practically to force his decree abolishing the *chador* and veil upon the reluctant women of his country. The chador is the long, enveloping gown designed to hide a woman's figure. After Reza Shah abdicated in 1942, the chador began making a comeback and is still widely worn in Iran.

In Pakistan many women walking in public are totally covered. They see through a strip of gauze sewn into an opening in the black hood covering their heads. When one asks why, the explanation is that the women prefer it this way. Faithfulness to a husband means total faithfulness.

However, younger girls are moving out more, abandoning the role of housewife for jobs in offices and businesses. This is due directly to increased educational opportunities and contact with foreigners. American-made motion pictures have also been credited with changing some of the age-old ideas about a woman's place in the world.

In Saudi Arabia, where the Wahabi sect is devoted to preserving the old traditions of Islam, there has recently been complaint that the influx of foreigners brought in to work on industrial projects is endangering Moslem ideals with heretical ideas.

THE WILL OF ALLAH

Islamic countries, in general, are in the best position they have been in for the past 150 years. The average Moslem views this current prosperity, international importance, and bright future as gifts of Allah. Moslems point to Sura 3 of the Koran as proof that this turn of fortune was expected and due:

And be not fainthearted, and be not sorrowful:
for ye shall gain the upper hand if ye be believers.

If a wound hath befallen you, a wound like it
hath already befallen others: we alternate these days
of successes and reverses among men, that
God may know those who have believed and that
He may take martyrs from among you.

GLOSSARY

Allah—The Moslem name for God.

Allahu Akbar—Arabic words, often used at the beginning of prayer, meaning, "God is most great."

Black Muslims—An American religious sect, composed of black people, who base their beliefs upon Islam.

Caliph—The name means "successor" and is given to the person who is the spiritual head of the Islamic religion.

Fatiha—A chapter from the Koran that is a popular Moslem prayer. It is often quoted by Moslems before going on a journey.

Hadith—Traditional stories about Mohammed and his first followers. These were gathered and preserved soon after Mohammed's death and provide much of what we know about the Prophet.

Hajj—The pilgrimage to Mecca that all good Moslems are urged to make at least once in their lifetime.

Imam—The title of the leader of prayer in the mosque. The Shiite sect call their spiritual leader imam instead of caliph.

Islam—The word means "submission to God." It is the religion of the Moslem people.

Jihad—Holy war. Moslems believe that if they fall while fighting for their religion, they go directly to paradise without waiting for Judgment Day.

Kaaba—The shrine and black meteoric stone in the city of Mecca. Islam teaches that it was given to Abraham by Allah. The Kaaba is of ancient origin and was worshiped by pagan Arabs before Mohammed preached Islam.

Koran—The Bible of Islam. Islam teaches that the Koran was dictated to Mohammed by the archangel Gabriel, and that it is an exact copy of a golden book preserved in heaven.

Mecca—The holy city of Islam located in western Saudi Arabia. None but Moslems are permitted to enter Mecca. All Moslems are urged to make a pilgrimage to Mecca at least once in their lifetime.

Medina—The second most holy Islamic city. Mohammed fled to Medina when driven from Mecca.

Mihrab—The alcove or niche in a mosque that shows the direction of Mecca. All prayers must be made with the face turned toward the holy city.

Minbar—The pulpit from which the imam leads the prayer in a mosque.

Moslem—The word means one who has submitted to God and is used to denote a person who believes and follows the religion of Islam.

Mosque—The Moslem place of worship. Although sermons are preached in the mosque, it is primarily a place for prayer.

Muezzin—The person appointed to call the faithful to prayer.

Quraysh—The Arabic tribe that controlled Mecca in Mohammed's day.

Rakah—Bowing down during prayer.

Salat—The daily Moslem prayers.

Shahalad—The reciting of the Creed of Islam.

Shiites—Followers of the Shia sect of Islam, founded by Ali.

Sufis—A Moslem mystic sect.

Sunnites—Followers of the Sunna sect of Islam. These are the orthodox Moslems.

Sura—A chapter of the Koran.

Ulama—Doctor of religious law.

Zakat—Almsgiving.

MEMORABLE DATES IN ISLAMIC HISTORY

A.D. 570   Birth of Mohammed
    595   Mohammed marries Khadija
    610   Archangel Gabriel appears to Mohammed
    622   The Hegira (Flight to Medina)

630	Mohammed captures Mecca
632	Mohammed dies in Medina
	Abu-Bakr elected First Caliph
634	Zaid begins assembling the Koran
	Abu-Bakr dies; Omar elected Second Caliph
637	Moslems win victories in Persia
644	Omar dies; Othman elected Third Caliph
656	Othman assassinated; Ali takes office as Fourth Caliph
	Kharijites form independent Islamic sect
661	Ali assassinated; Muawiyah becomes caliph by force
711	Ommiad caliphs complete invasion of North Africa and invade Spain
732	Moslem invasion of France stopped at Tours
1099	Crusaders drive Moslems from Jerusalem
1187	Saladin recaptures Jerusalem during Third Crusade
1258	Mongols capture Baghdad
1326	Beginning of Ottoman Empire
1492	Ferdinand and Isabella expel Moslems from Spain
1519	Mogul Empire established in India by Baber
1757	British conquest of India begins, ultimately to end Moslem rule in India
1914	Ottoman caliph joins Germany in World War I
1920	Britain and France receive League of Nations mandates to govern sections of Middle East
1923	Kemel Ataturk forms Republic of Turkey, ending Ottoman Empire
1945	End of World War II begins breakup of colonial empires, leading to independence of Moslem countries
1976	Estimated number of world Moslems: 529,108,700

FOR FURTHER READING

Bake, Liva. *World Faiths*. New York: Abelard-Schuman, 1965.

Editorial Staff of *Life*. *The World's Great Religions*. New York: Simon & Schuster, 1958.

Fitch, Florence Mary. *Allah, the God of Islam*. New York: Lothrop, Lee & Shepard, 1950.

Gaer, Joseph. *Young Heroes of the Living Religions*. Boston: Little, Brown & Co., 1953.

While not written for young readers, the following is one of the more complete biographies of Mohammed:

Rodinson, Maxime. *Mohammed*. New York: Pantheon Books, 1971.

Two standard translations of the Koran are:

Dawood, N. J. *The Koran*. Harmondsworth (England): Penguin Classics, 1974.

Rodwell, J. M. *The Koran*. London: Everyman's Library, 1909 (first translated in 1861).

INDEX